Language of Water
Language of Fire
a celebration of lesbian and gay poetry

Here is a collection of poems from every corner of the British Isles. They celebrate a diamond of many facets — the Lesbian and Gay Community. These poets, as many before them and also those who were not included in this book, are writing our history.

It has been a great pleasure working with these poets, whose flexibility and co-operation have made this anthology possible. Special thanks extends to those who by contributing to this volume have shown great strength in defying those who would rather we were silent. They have The Language Of Water, The Language Of Fire.

Berta Freistadt & Pat O'Brien, 1992

D1208398

The Oscars Press, BM Oscars, London WC1N 3XX.
Distribution: Turnaround, 27 Horsell Road, London N5 1XL, UK and Inland
Book Co, PO Box 120261, 140 Commerce St, East Haven, CT 06512, USA.

Cover photograph: Gordon Rainsford.
Cover design: Derek John Hood and Martin Butterworth.
Typesetting by Counter Productions, London.
Printed and bound by Billing & Sons, Worcester.
The Oscars Press is a member of the Association of Little Presses and the
Small Press Group.

Financially assisted by London Arts Board.

Also published by the Oscars Press:
Take Any Train: a book of gay men's poetry, edited by Peter Daniels
Whatever You Desire: a book of lesbian poetry, edited by Mary Jo Bang
Of Eros and Of Dust: poems from the city, edited by Steve Anthony

Language of Water
Language of Fire

a celebration of lesbian and gay poetry

Edited by
Berta Freistadt and Pat O'Brien

PoetryConsultant
Ken King

ACKNOWLEDGEMENTS

Thankyou to Gregory Woods for 'Hereafter' from his forthcoming collection *We Have The Melon* (Carcanet 1992); Dene Reynolds for 'Muscle Bound In Condom Skin' that appeared in *Square Peg* (No.28); Peter Daniels for 'Construction', published in *Cargo* (Australia) and 'Hunger', which appears in *Scratch*; Martin Humphries for 'The Sheer Mindless Brutality Of It', published in the first anthology of gay mens' poetry to be published in the U.K - *Not Love Alone* (GMP 1985); Dinyar Godrej for 'Everything Is Agreed Upon' from a collection of his work in *Twentysomething* (GMP 1992); Paul Boakye for '2000 Seasons', taken from his play *Boy With Beer*; Aspen for her poem 'Bitter And Twisted', recently published in *Disability Arts Magazine*.

CONTENTS

Language of Water, Language of Fire
Errata:
The text of Elizabeth Carola's *Milk Anyone?* which appears on page 68 of this volume is an uncorrected proof. As this contains several stylistic and typographical errors, we enclose the correct version of this poem – with apologies to the poet.

ELIZABETH CAROLA

Milk Anyone?

The topic of tonight's discussion is Battered Lesbians.
The lighting's sort of harsh, you note.
You think to make the tea.

"We need to acknowledge the importance of the issue"
— milk anyone?
"Not to be afraid to make the links"
— and sugar?
"We need an analysis. A committee. A public forum. A refuge…"
— I know you like yours strong, so here

When her arm flung across you in sleep
an almost itinerant tenderness
was the tie that bound you thinly to the world

When her eyes went coal and you waited for it
sudden   *that's it bitch you've had it now*   unknowable
shocking you only   into stronger resolve
to anticipate   be more prepared   **to get it right next time**

When violent misery was the air you breathed,
seemed to settle the whole estate in a fine, steely dust
and you leant over the balcony quiet moments,
knowing it was the same in all the flats, women
putting up   shutting up   dodging blows   screaming back
but imagining a place   one flat maybe
where tenderness was the way

You held this flat in your mind like a prayer.
And at night, half asleep, when you moved together
and her body relented   let you back in
you *knew* you could make it   the one

The women are talking Battered Lesbians.
Having nothing to say, you serve out more tea
drink yours   three sugars   slow.

ANNIE BLUE

This tumult of words,
wild
as a thousand
silent waterfalls,
rushing and rolling,
tossing and fading,
cascading into caverns;

glimpsed and lost,
glimpsed and lost,

tumbling away formless
and flowing towards
some other distant island.
Lover...
what is between us
will remain unsaid,
until we learn
the language of water.

This brilliance of words,
bright
as a midnight field
of fire-flies,
flickering and glowing,
dancing and vanishing,
bursting into flame;

blazing and dying,
blazing and dying,

falling away dreamlike
and fading in the shadows
of countless ghostly fires.
Lover...
what we feel
must remain untold,
until we learn
the language of fire.

ELEANOR DARE

Delirious on Cider Barrel ice
lollies and Old Holborn, you
always were a poof in a lime
green mohican walking with
a child dyke, well - half
a child. Maybe it was 2 am
then Matthew, it was 2 am
most times. In that slice of
town none of the women knew
how to be my friend, no one did
until you came along - with a
bag full of Crazy Colours and
torn magazines. You taught
me how to snatch at life - to
call my negaholic father a
tight old turd. You even tried to
teach me how to cruise... another story
On Sundays we'd drink Pinacoladas
in your bombsite room while your
(Reverend) father worked late
at the church. I'd sit by the
window reading Spare Rib or
Sylvia Plath while you'd lie on
the bed wanking over Zipper or
a record cover with a patch of
male skin. We were criminals -
but I'm wilder now. I wonder
if you are even alive - did I
teach you anything Matthew?
Ten years on I've met Dykes I
like better than I ever liked you.
None of them taught me how to find
drugs or bunk off from school. It's
2 am now Matthew - once it was
2 am most times and all the dykes
I know are in bed before you.

GREGORY WOODS

Skin

From 20-hole DMs
with toecaps scuffed as if
on a mendicant's teeth

to his No 1 crop,
his menaces had the
effect on me he meant,

but I could taste a fear
beneath the sweetness of
his recondite tattoos.

When whetted torchbeams scraped
the shadow of his pelt,
he ordered me to shut

the blinds. He had to gag
himself against the least
expression of delight.

What became of the flesh?
There are no relics in
the quicklime of my heart.

When he left before dawn
the bedroom windows were
weeping like beauty queens.

Hereafter

The dead porn boy is still
doing it, coming time
and again as if taken
    by surprise,

no better prepared than
the innocent he looks
for this convulsion of
    old pleasures.

From his raucous breath and
the sticky glamour of
his belly, we who watch
    him glean our

unlikely luck, compelled to
remember him each time,
oblivious, he wets our
    handkerchiefs.

In time his repertoire
of masks will seem rehearsed,
refined, impulsive as
    kabuki,

and we'll have taught ourselves
to duplicate his gestures
out of deference to the
    tradition.

But unlike the Jesus
weltering in sweat on
a gold chain across his
    collar bone,

we won't get any nearer
godliness than when he
spreads his legs and lifts his
    shaggy arse.

VIV ACIOUS

i want to be a Dandy when i grow up.
Not a comic figure,

                    but a true professional cad –
a jack the lad amongst women.

          When i grow up – pah!
i AM grown – an ungrown, unknown adult.

    Besuited, i would send flowers daily
          to all of my friends,
  and spend days composing poignant messages on
    poignant cards
            and send them gaily
   immersed in my favourite scent
               so that that person
   would feel me beside them,
                a subliminal reality
   a sensual delight.

I'd be foppish and camp
and completely philanthropic. Wine and dine the
pleasures mine.

I would however, need money to do all these things.

OH to be a dandy.

MARIE BERCĚ

Susan Perry

My red trike and your hawthorn tree equalled magic
We roamed the back fields together, making dens and telling stories

Then you moved to Flixton and I was disappointed, when I stayed,
   that we had to share a bedroom with your brothers.
And when you stayed at my house you got homesick, crying into
   your scrambled egg and tomato.

Later, you took to horseriding
Put me through misery when I rode bareback just to please you
And complained about plastic handbags
Only leather was good enough for you!

What happened to you after you stopped being engaged to a
   policeman?

Are you a dyke yet?

I want to go to your house in the middle of the night and watch you
   sleeping

Sweet dreams!

SARAH DELAWNEY

I'll come out tomorrow
I'll tell 'em I'm bent
Tomorrow came and lingered
Tomorrow came and went.

Imagine their reactions!
Imagine what they'd say!
If I told them that their daughter
Was absolutely gay.

Picture now their faces!
Surprise? Guilt? Shame?
Replaced by surging anger,
A fire from a flame.

They'd reject me and they'd spurn me
They'd grow to hate my face,
They'd treat me like an outcast
A stranger to their race.

I'll come out tomorrow,
I'll tell 'em I'm bent,
Tomorrow came and lingered,
Tomorrow came and went.

DEBBIE HAMBLEY

Alone I Am Insignificant - But Together We Are Recognized

Here I sit in the
Sixth form lounge at school.
Me, alone - an insignificant being.
I sit alone at the table,
Other friends elsewhere in
The lounge.

But then I suppose
Us Lesbians have always
Been insignificant; or
Maybe not so much insignificant
As unacknowledged.
Whether it be in education,
Work or society as a whole!

I'm sick of being so
Insignificant, ignored and
Unrecognized by society.
I am me, I'm a woman
And I just happen to be
A Lesbian, too. And I want
To be recognized as all 3!

But when we Lesbians or
Gay men get together at Pride,
Lark in the Park and other such
Times.
Then we are no longer
Insignificant, we are here and
We are many, and no one is
Able to ignore our existence!

14

JAN SELLERS

It was you

Elves are for children, but you
green-eyed, adult, lean and brown
smiling, luminous
dangerous

bring memory back.
You couldn't have known

it was you I was waiting for
those long, hot, indolent summers

making love to myself in the long wild grasses
guilt growing domestic as daisies
pleasure budding

☆

I always hoped the elves might carry me off.
Wilful, I slept under may trees

taked to oak trees
(no-one answered back)

lingered late at dusk;
dawdled in the park.

They said, the goblins will get you
I wanted it to be elves
knew I was different
waited

never knew it would be you

RYAN GILBEY

Two Ages

(one)

the boys in the stall
giggled and groped
with tender glovepuppet hands
young, too young
to be there:
those firecrackerfingers
and buttocks clenched tight
as the teeth of a vice:
the murmuring, the loosening
    of belts and crotches,
tugging at silk shorts, members
stirring in the fabric
t-shirts hoisted over
    ruffled blonde heads
ribs strain and brother
in milky skin.
    then they saw him:
the loiterer
the uglypapa
the rudehybrid
in the corner where the ladies
do their faces.

    when they're your age
they'll know what it is
to dread waking
with feet like hands
and eyes like sphincters
in a bed that gets bigger
with every absent friend.

    when they're your age
they'll loathe
the crackle of bacon

the obesity of sausages
in a stranger's kitchen
the indigestion of gulping
the embarrassment of leaving
and the futility
of tomorrow's breakfast
in another kitchen.
     when they're your age
they'll break the codes of youth
with leather slippers
fruit preserve
dressing-gowns
and socks in bed
they will leer on fire-escapes
in longjohns
yellowed by tobacco
at your age decay will greet them
like a prizefighter's swing.
     but in your blackest
            heart of hearts
you know they will never see
your age
they will be granted
the mercy of young death:
cherries plucked
in gorgeous icy ripeness
before the maggot spoils
for God protects the beautiful
and gentlemen prefer blondes.

     scrape off the mascara
to reveal the mascara;
take a scalpel to the fiend
and see the fiend;
peel the woman away
down to the man
and likewise
the man to the woman.

     to offer
a lift to a runaway

it could entrap a purity
a dignity
an illegal tenderness
oh, at that age
the silk sheets and champagne
would have numbed your brain
into sweet submission.

(two)

      the hitchhiking thumb is rude
and stumpy aloft it beckons
(remember at Aunt Pamela's party
why, you were only a young thing
of seven,
a sprout of a lad
still waking to the humid sheen
and stench of yellow bedsheets
and you returned from a solitary
visit to the lavatory
with your peeping-olive pee-pee
poking out like
      an uncertain pronunciation
they laughed
and they laughed
but no-one laughs anymore
                    in the dark)
      and loitering at the roadside
just a scrap of a thing
— the limousine purrs
you cross yourself and enter
the clouds roll on
with the rumble and leisure
of bowling-balls in the alley
where ten pounds in a johnnie
and a large coca-cola
            made you happy
for the first time
and it may have been the last time
but you're always on the look-out

for the next time.
        there is darkness inside
and a great divide
between the driver and the driven –
a wall of glass ensures
opportunity for introductions
in the muted familiarity of
the long leather backseat beach –
see how his talon-hand
            of skinless fingers
                is already upon you!
        here – the plasticity of your host –
the make-up poorly disguises
the creases of the skin,
    crumbled and deflated
            as an overripe pear
the lips, artistry spent and cracked
                like a restoration masterwork
the rigid suit, the unrumpled shirt,
the strains of corset outlined there,
the sincerity of
    the sincerity in his eyes.
            he will engulf your youth
your unblemished form,
he will suck at your nipples
'til they're as black
                and hung as his
and the envy of your soft thick cock
will drive him to shave your crotch
or kill himself
or both;
your favours will write you
            into his will
but you shall grow old and seasoned
waiting for the sombre shadow
to drift towards his bedside
and claim him.
        but he promises to make you happy
though it won't be for the first time
and it might not be the last time
there's nothing to say

that it won't be the best time.
     the sun slips shamefully away
and nighteyes blink into life
like whore-bulbs in the darkness
     though sex may be
the classless tool
you, boy,
have the power
to make grown men weep
              and drool...
turn off the light now
for something sobs
and calls

Tenderfoot

the boy skirts around
the nucleus of boys —

he wants one but
he doesn't know which one
he wants the most

he found a mirror
and saw himself in it

he heard a whisper —
a voice was writ within it

now he has a voice
he needs a megaphone

he knows fresh love —
he spent so long alone

the knot of bodies
ripples and parts

teasing and tempting
they permit him to join
and strengthen the fist

for the next novice
on the circumference

KRISH SADHANA

Lesbian Moon

There is a strange moon
That excites me
Beyond the call
Of any lunar madness

To wear hats
Inside my knickers
And develop relationships
With small pink feathers

Strolling through a
Shower of nipples
I miss the bus
Again and again and again and again and again

Little curly hairs
Invade my pockets
At awkward moments
Giving the game away

Gay Parenting

"Its a boy!" cried Tonto
Softly looking down at his son
"Next time you get to be the mother"
        Said an irritable Lone Ranger.

TIMOTHY GALLAGHER

Barry Tells

I have a feeling that among your many talents is that of the sculptor.
I have observed that you don't seem to know what to do with your
hands.
I have a feeling you are keen to do me. Well, here I am. Potentially,
your magnum opus.

Is it the exhibitionist in me that drives me to it? Yes. But then it's
more than that. It's spring. Which means I am at a loss. Which means I
have this need to shed certain inapplicable items of clothing for the
benefit of a sensitive, appreciative stranger.
This is not to say I am not self-conscious.
This is not to say I cannot be coy.
This is not to say my body is not festering.

Please have me as your model... As one of your models?
I promise to make the most of my chance.
I promise not to get in the way.
I promise to be whatever you want me to be.

It isn't a mirror I'm after. Mirrors are too big, accommodate too many
things.

If you accept me as your model – as one of your models? – I'll do
whatever you want. If you want, I'll make love with myself as you
capture me in whatever is your preferred substance.
I have a feeling this will improve the look of me.

Naturally, I'll need your assistance, your example. I'll need to see you,
naked.

Oh you artists. You are impossible.
How insubstantial your are. There's really nothing to you.
I like that. I like the prospect that, as you do your sculpture, you are
fading away.

Please, don't take that personally.

Please, do not dismiss me.
I promise to take nothing for granted.
I promise to be your prize model.
I promise to be beautiful before it is too late.

DENE REYNOLDS

Muscle Bound In Condom Skin

Muscle sheathed in condom skin;
Silk
Tight
Bound in clumps.
Thick smooth syrup chest
Muscles bound in condom skin.
Your beautiful, awesome, silent, naked
Black oil hair
Satin and wet
From the thoughtful forehead
To the nape of the neck.
Muscle bound in tight rubber sock
(with translucent lubricant);
Dark
Dark
Dark treacle skin
Shine pearlescent droplets
Of salt water and best friends spunk;
Salt water and best friends spunk.

NANCY WHITE

Epiphany

The first time I slept with a woman
I felt like the young Errol Flynn
Proud as punch and twice as drunk
But without the moustache
I smiled down at that live girl
Hooped in my arms
Sighing naked rosy breaths
She had it all and so did I

I asked her if
she would and
she said

'The first time I slept with a woman
I didn't sleep at all
But was visited by divine inspiration
And knew just what to do'

Then her whole body twirled
On the tip of my finger
And the choirs of angels gasped.
You see, there is no going back.

BERNADETTE HALPIN

after a swim

Lick, you said, the salt from my skin;
I want you to. My tongue obeyed and drew
a vein darker than your skin (dark
as sunned sand) and deep:
a track, a line, language below
our last estranging conversation.
Your taste stings in my mouth —
and they seem too far again those long hours —
salt burning my eyes, flowing
in harsh desire against my fingers.
I licked them then and thought of you.
Now I am shaping the cool circle where
your breast weighs like windfall soft fruit
heaviest. Its milk is a sweet flood that bathes
my wounded and recalcitrant tongue.

TRACIE PEISLEY

Juicy Fruiters

This is about my sweetheart, my sweet thang, my girl lover, my friend; my tender, giving, musk smelling damson. This is about her tongue in my mouth, lolling, loving it all, a thick pink muscle, tense and sweet, with her taste, her smell, my gem, my jewel, wear you upon my head like a big old floppy hat; She, in my face, in my hair, her bigness over me, like a warm day, like another world. Delirium, running her tongue across my eyelids, hmmmm, like a tear drop has fallen there, like a wish, like I don't know how, like her hands running up and down me, up and down me, into every God-damn single crease and tender part, all tender parts of me exposed for her, my delicious vulnerability, making me fizz up inside, making me cry out. This is about my lady, my lady friend; taking my toes in her mouth, with small hands and large teeth, her tongue there again, too much now I can't believe it, between my toeses, rolling away from her, kicking the air, hand still in her hair pulling, wriggling, delighted, laughing, the sheet like a sail in our legs, hysterical now, yelping like pups, the sound beating about our heads. Grabbing handfuls of her, stuffing her into my mouth, like a big cream horn, like she's covered in chocolate or something; can I devour her? can I become her? can I eat her up? Her screaming into my neck, my name, sending a sort of shuddering through me, my toes tightly curled, wet between my legs now, of course! My downy hairs smothering her damp curls, carefree fingering. Too much now, aching but familiar, like an old old fairy story, like an old resting place, old roosters, juicy fruiters, heaving each other all over the floor, like some lumbering animal, like big bananas, like we always are, shameless, sweet!

DAVID SEMPLE

Love Sonnets To A Vegan, Numbers 1 & 2

1.
Is this the way it's always going to be? Your black coffee,
My white tea. On walnut chairs, we rock and creak,
Mine soft leather and yours hard teak. You'll make yourself old,
Punishing your pelvis for the sake of your soul.
Your locust protest. Your kidney bean dream. When the fly
   crashlands
In your coffee cup, you say a mass. And I throw up.

A pale pin-cushion bean-pole, raw chalk eyes and lips,
I could post you in a pillar box, I could stack plates in your ribs.
Arms like bedsheets in the breeze, billowing for love.
Your glass slipper is a crucifix, fits you like a glove.
You've cancelled fame and fortune for the role of Cinderella,
In your sacred ashen overcoat you look like an umbrella.
Marching for mosquitoes, saving the hammerhead shark,
You'll get yourself in the history books, but only as a bookmark.

2.
Is this the way it's always going to be? Fighting over
Dairy products. Vitalite and U.H.T.
Honey equals slavery, woolly jumper equals theft,
I know I'm just a tyrant, and maybe you know best
But if I roll over in bed tonight I'll crush you in my sleep,
You'll be a sticky imprint, just a shadow on the sheets.

A three-year love turns into a pressed lily overnight,
Very ozone-friendly. But not a pretty sight.
I'm sorry I don't share your faith, I'll see what I can do,
I will eat lentil casserole, I will wear plastic shoes,
And chew organic carrots, gherkins, artichokes and capers,
And type this poem out again on recycled paper.
And pray that Mother Earth will save the planet, deliver us,
Now let's turn the lights off and get carnivorous.

ROSIE HUDSON

I am a crab
and I live in a shell on the beach.

Sometimes
I go for a walk.

I walk to the sea
and enter the raging waters
that boom and crash
and pull and smash
all around me.

I go out — deep, deep —
and I swim.

There are treasures out there.
Colour.
And life.
Moving and flowing
and living and growing and dying.

I watch for a while
trying to understand
an inner reality.

Sometimes I do.
And sometimes I don't.

And then
when I feel ready
I turn
and swim back to the shore
and walk from the lapping waters
onto the beach again.

I lie
turn my face to the sky
and think.

CATHY BOLTON

Against The Tide

The sea erases my steps
From the damp, squeaky sand.

Black gulls rise and fall
In the belly of the bleeding sun.

My nail traces, retraces
The grooves of a shell.

Waves swell about my ankles
Their darkness lures.

Half-naked, white frills
Gather around my waist.

An invitation so vast
It tastes of oblivion.

Anchored, my feet resist
The beat of a thousand oars.

STEVE ANTHONY

In The Pool

He lies back in the pool, perfectly
   still, his arms floating free,
      the water unbroken

but for the tiny outcrops of his nipples
   and the fine skyline of his face,
      watching the waterlight

swim on the ceiling. I grip the handrail,
   out of my depth. As he hoists himself up,
      I take in his body

from the swell of his calves
   to the broad harbour of his back.
      I could rest forever there.

Under the shower, his head thrown back,
   I'm a drop of water riding his skin.
      He turns. Our eyes meet.

When I'm dressed, he's disappeared.

The Gift

It was Auden that gave me away, you said,
Alone in the carriage at the end of the line,
Pretending to read. Later, our bed
The golf course, under the moon

And the jittery leaves, you asked my name,
First, before we kissed, undressed.
I could barely see your face, though your frame
Was clear against the grass, and I guessed

I might never meet you again. But stretched
On the well-kept lawn that summer night,
Two strangers shared each other, touched —
A gift essential as love, or sight.

Table For One

Even an avocado's made for two,
sharing itself so openly;

food's version of foreplay,
appetiser to the feast.

As I savour one now, I see you
scooping your favourite fruit

and smiling up at me, happy —
like you were that long afternoon

in some out-of-season hotel,
where we emptied the day of everything

but ourselves, and were satisfied.
I'm left with a hollow skin.

TESSA HANKINSON

Long fuck, slow fuck, sweet fuck, deep fuck.
Hard fuck, eyes locked intense fuck – inches from my face fuck.

Clutching at a headboard, straining under the onslaught.
Trying to squeeze a little more of her in, just a little
bit harder, for a little while longer.

Alone At The Bell

I strained to see Sal in the woman and curse
her for being a stranger taunting me with
similarities.
So near, yet not there at all. A mirage.
A carefully constructed illusion. Reach out
and touch – and she disappears into the bottom
of your glass.
A nice girl, someone called Melonie perhaps,
or Jane.
Baggy shorts, Sal's dance but with less grace,
an awkward mover who thought she had style.
I passed her in the loo and took a second look.
Too young, chin too narrow, cheap looking vest.
Back in the disco I turn to watch the queue and
the clock creeping ever further towards a time too
late for her to come and when the straggling line
finally goes I drain my glass stumbling to the bar.

LIANN SNOW

One Day

We lingered at the water's side
You beyond a wall
Smiling childlike on the ledge.

You thought me near at hand
Divided only by the stone
Prepared to talk with you unseen,
But I ranged far
Along the sloped embankment;
Leaned with serious pleasure
Against the curving rocks beneath my feet,
And gazed below at water;
Then stared, as if a mariner,
At distant towns
Which lay along the river's edge.

I heard your voice
Distantly, not doubting I would come.
I would not let my heart respond,
But waited, seated on the stone
For the change in tone.

I heard the stronger need
Expressed in altered sound
And tore wild flowers rootless
From the soil
And brought you them.

MANDY DEE

Inconsistency

Flee! fly from between my inconsistent hands!
Nip quick thro' my fingers
Lest I squash you in my palms

Last week I'd picked you from my jug
You were viscous with liquid
Crushed by the great weight of water.
I thought your minimal movement
was the lurch of the dead-drowned.
Yet as massive droplets drained off the pencil's edge
Your wing tips flicked sticky from your sides
from my vast jug of waters
you had returned; alive

I had watched the lampheat break into your saturated form
Intensely possessive
arrogant with love;
I wondered would my sudden impulse
allow you to survive?
As paralysis faded from your joints
Your whole frame shuddered and stepped out into flight

But now I know
Some day I'll lie paralysed
While you or yours have life to fly
whether you'll live or die you'll never see
my gargantuan face beneath your many eyes
you'll not notice me!
So you'd better flee now,
fly!
and I'm angry now,
so I slap my hands together.

Fly! ...are you crushed;
Have you died?

STEVE CRANFIELD

Being In A Relationship

Being in a relationship
is meeting every third question
with an answer that begins: "When you're in a relationship…"

Being in a relationship
is wanting to astonish other people with:
"He cooked this really wonderful meal last night."

Being in a relationship
is shopping for two
and buying one-and-a-half times more than the pair of you need.

Being in a relationship
is mainly an affair
of waiting for the other person.

Being in a relationship
is staying at home and telling lonely friends:
"You should get out more."

Being in a relationship
is remaining open
to the possibility.

Being in a relationship
is excusing yourself from this year's Pride march:
"Work's been a bitch, and we need some time together,

away from the crowd,
to build up our relationship."
For "relationship" read "holiday tan".

Drugs and AIDS Workshops, Budapest, November 1990

A Trainer's Notes

for Jean Faugier

No paper, no chalk,
no room: we train three days in
a bowling alley.

Bulgaria tests
millions: 28 sailors
(one port) HIV.

At dinner, Thatcher
deposition jokes fall flat.
The Czechs keep eating.

A Slovak doctor —
bearded, jeans — revives spirits
of May '68.

Dr Szykorska
longs for a Poland free from
poppy straw and priests.

Three Bulgarians
produce some home-made cognac.
They've no flight home booked.

"Hungarians should
fuck just with Hungarians."
"Including gypsies?"

I have learnt to feel —
I have learnt to understand —
I have learnt skills of —

VALERIE HARWOOD

Bouquet 148 Hours Passed

winter is her, clouds are dark
i lie blanket wrapped
hidden from the world
dreaming of a whisper that said goodnight

i close my dark lids
halos to hide from the sun
watching flowers he gave you
peeling
day by day outward moving
unfolding shadows to silhouette my wall

she walks in the wind
her clothes tease my daydreams
i see her dark hair dance in the night
remembering her promises
watching myself make love in the gardens
i left for her

full moon paints nightshade images
animation sinks to the floor
crinkled life in the vase of thorns
he gave me
she is moving beside me
i am clutching empty garments
bed a tourniquet
you are with him tonight echoes his lovemaking
beating funeral rhythms against my mind

i am a woman
alone with the nightingale
concealed beneath thick white sheets
upon which the gales of memory
permit no dust to settle

MICHAEL RUSSOFF

Great Expectations

(An elegy to the moon)

When small, I longed to disturb your surface,
Prod you like a chocolate cake,
Imagining how you felt to touch, to taste.

I watched the way you bared yourself and
Took my cue from you: drew on your
brightness, as on a lighted cigarette,

Yet did not understand then how the
Cold could burn as well. Grown
Older now, I see how similar we are:

Two ghosted shells, and both so full of years.
Tonight, you are the largest tear in my eye:
Wombed by my sorrows, they were my griefs that

Gave you your birth, spat you out above the earth.
Varnished by your light, I lie here
Stranded as the worm in summer:

Distance lied, the grass verge now unreachable.

CATHY BOLTON

Scared Of Heights

I was disappointed
When you lowered your
Stubborn weight to the ground
And said I can't go on.
I hate turning back
Without the taste of victory on my lips.
The air was too thin,
It made you dizzy.
But I love that feeling,
Pushing my face into the wind,
Gasping for breath,
Then floating in bright colours.

You were disappointed
When my body buckled
Beneath your warm skin
And I said I can't go on.
You hate turning back
Without the cry of ecstasy in your ear.
The thrill was too intense,
It scared me.
But you love that feeling,
Pushing your body into oblivion,
Gasping for breath,
Then floating in bright colours.

DAVID CRITCHARD

More Than Mere Absence

In memoriam Brian Gregory

"Table for one, sir?"
                              "Please."

Shown to a table for two,
I sit staring at emptiness,
as recent memories replay,
uncontrolled:
                    "Tickets for the play?"
"Just one thanks."
                              "O yes, of course."

"I'll see you on Saturday."
                              "Gosh!
You're coming to the party by yourself?"
"Of course."
                    "That's brave, so soon….."
(does he mean brazen, really?)

In the busy restaurant
smoke-filled air almost congeals
into something more painful,
more palpable then mere absence.

Unaware, the chattering diners sit
and do not see the ghost-void opposite.

Shared Laughter

*For Winifred, on the anniversary of Margaret's death, which was
also the anniversary of my lover Brian's death*

Well,
it's been a year now, and we've coped somehow.
It is the laughter that we miss the most.

However busy or however bad the day,
something would bring
that wicked chuckle to our throats.

We still think,
"We must tell them that when we get home"
and find
we have to laugh alone.

Boxes

In memoriam Brian Gregory

He kept all his past in boxes
neatly stacked
from floor to ceiling of a room
he never used.

Now it is my job to sort them
and give away
or sell those pegs of memory
he couldn't lose.

The one box that he never saw
now waits for me.
One summer day I'll pour its contents
in the sea.

The final disposition that he chose
will be for me
a memory that I can never lose.

43

Colourscapes

Following Gertrude Jekyll
and Vita Sackville-West, she said,
"My garden will be but a single colour."

It took very little effort to eliminate
the wishy-washy yellow of the primroses,
the orange of the marigolds and wallflowers.

Most of the garden then was blue,
except for the tenacious poppies
and an old red rose that bloomed again.

After much effort, she succeeded.
But, by self-seeding, the purple-blue
always seemed to change to lavender:
the paler blues degenerated into pink.
It puzzled her. "Genetics," someone said.
Having been but briefly an indifferent chemist,
she could not come to terms with that.

VICKY BLAKE

Police said 20,000
Organisers said 40,000
Worried I went to the police
"Police" I said "I want to make out a missing persons report"
"Yes madam" he said
I said "20,000 gay men and lesbians on the afternoon of the 29th June
in Central London"
He said "Are you taking the piss?"
I said "To lose one gay man or lesbian may be regarded as a severe
misfortune
to lose 20,000 looks like carelessness"

Balancing the Books

Walking down the street
A solicitor   A professional
Walking down the street
Dicks on building site mouthing off.
Oh, but of course, how silly of me to forget
When I'm walking down the street
I'm tits and arse and walking cunt
How silly of me to forget.
Marching down the street
On another day
The drag queens are out
Resplendent in the sun.
Earrings twinkling
Mouthing off.
Dicks on a building site
Stunned into beetroot silence.

Such joy!
The wild justice of Revenge
and
Life Balancing the Books

PETER DANIELS

Construction

Out on the busy street one morning, dust in the air.

Grey-bearded God stood in his pinstripe suit and
a battered red construction helmet. He winked
behind his sunglasses: you failed to notice,
concentrating on a simple tune, balancing a few
basic rules of engineering. But then a fact
entered your eye: a speck of diamond. The path
of his eyebeam refracted through his
dark perspex at a critical angle to hit
your own beam bouncing off the surface.

And you became aware of the Divine Presence.

"Here it is", said God — in his camp male stance with
the knack of irony — "find it." You were looking
lost-all-alone in a pair of pretty red
steel-capped shoes. Where was the correct
posture to answer his narcissistic challenge?
It's unheroic to rehearse the jargon, though it's fun
trying on the costumes. No good... No use... Ah, just
right - but the mess this place is in, and only
the laws of physics to cope with it.

The glamour of classification. sorting the gems.

We enjoy it. The minor flaws in perfected
blueprints blow up to grand holes in production.
The workday satisfaction is in mending them,
or blowing up the whole thing (demolition
is another subject with its own axioms).
To cultivate the instinct and the glittering eyes,
plan your clothes for work, ensuring health
and safety at all times: but the goal is
to build naked office blocks, in open-toed feet.

Hunger

Eating has been leaving me hollow
for a man born creating
new appetites, raising desires, fucking
his home from home. He's finding
his way, always leaving
unfinished business: reaching
for more than one requiring
more of him. Watch him building
a naked art form, letting it lift. Gulping
it in. A need the size of Glasgow

but London-greedy. Yes, you. Mouth full of
native tongue, but you make yourself
understood. When it arises, we hold it
how it comes, how we like it. But it's
holding only a snatched handful of
days from a year and both of us
insatiable — better put it away. It's
getting impossible. Let's give it up.

I walk home cold at midnight, past the baker's:
breathe in the warm emotion of yeast
rousing a cloud of half-satisfied
hunger, creating itself.

HELEN SALKIN

On Friday Nights

On Friday nights
I think about bread,
the plaited sort with a sweet taste
and two candles that
'light up the darkness and
drive away all evil'
but when I finish work
I stop outside the station
and buy flowers.

I carry them home
through all the people
and put them on your table
in place of bread and candles
and your smile
lights up my heart
and kindles my soul.

Havera

(Havera *Hebrew, fem.*: lover, friend, comrade.)

you hold me gently
as I clench my fists and teeth
and mutter, 'damn her, damn her, damn her'
into your luxuriant hair
till your arms tighten
bracing yourself for an explosion
has our god forsaken me
I lean into your strength
and forget to feel foolish

MAGGIE FORD

I want to say, Just once more my love
once more.
let me drown in your thighs
taste the sweet flesh of your breasts
wind my fingers through your hair
let them trail into the centre of the world
the spun bud of my love.
Is this pain as old as life?
Did Sappho burn as I do?
did her love for golden girls
in a world of men and heroes
simply pass unobserved unacknowledged?
How can you lose what in the
world's eyes does not exist?
My love, My love is dead
but for the world, it never lived.

In Memoriam

I open a drawer and find one of your socks.
A sad thing, shredded at the edges
faded and pointless without its partner.
Perhaps if I hold it close to me
take it to bed, pretend I'm its mate
it won't feel so unwanted.
Perhaps it will learn to survive
A solitary sock
hanging loose
in a world full of pairs.

MICHAEL VERINO

Love-Feast

You
god–damned
savage
sadistic
son of a bitch,
by every sick yellow male cell
may you become father to monsters which
will turn and rend you with jaws of steel,
little dagger teeth,
crush your bones,
bake them as a marrow cake,
boil your blood into soup
plumped with bobbing dumplings of buttocks fat,
fix a salad of your shining hair,
         your polished nails,
         your tattooed skin,
hoist your eyeballs on toothpicks,
a succulent jaundiced vision to the tongue.
Thus, lover,
I conjure up a feast of you —

like the one
you made
of me.

ANONYMOUS

A day in march
medals and gold
flaxen hair
brushing over
dust from the top
uniform of the sea
as blue as
your eyes darting
beneath the waves
of the sheets
the boots I unlace
and remove caressing
the soft butt
of my rifle
slowly sliding down
the skirts
of these anchored parts
I unbutton
my mouth
I am obedient
and loyal
I shall always do my duty
to you
my Majesty

JO FISK

Aunt Alice's 90th - Meeting the Other Dyke

Line up before Alice – ninety today   not that she knows it.
She used to drive trucks in the war.   From the '40s on is a blank now:
Each of us stop briefly   stilted mid carpet.

Introduced as child of my father.
Then shifted by mid queue impatience.

Searching in vain for whisky, I am stopped by a distant relative:
'This is Jane from Boston (the one I was looking out for).   This is Jo.'

Jane is Alice's child by one of her dead husbands.
Years ago she sounded exciting.
Bent – and not in prison.   An unexplained puzzle.

Nothing on ears and neck.   High heels, swollen feet.
Puffy fingers stretch towards me.   The ring is there – on the last
finger.

Restrained smile.   Jaw clenched.
Coldly brushing eyes over my neck she lurches past, feet in protest.

Standing in a vacuum of being snubbed by those who hate my absent
    mother,
heavy arms comfort my shoulders.
Jane is back with her roommate, 'Meet my cousin Jo.'

PETER WYLES

"One Of Them"

No straight man wants a gay son.
There's none of that in me at all.
I'd always assumed he'd find a nice girl
marry, settle down. I want grandchildren

but it's his life. I'll stand by him.

His mother says we shouldn't ask
"Where we went wrong." I suppose that's right.
I don't like any of the words it's called by.
We've barely discussed it, since that phone-call.

No matter. I love him. He's still my son.
We had his friend down for Christmas
a nice lad, shy, joined in the fun.
The two of them look happy together.

He's better now he's told us, younger.
There's so much worry, being a father,
three bright lads, all with their problems
still hanging over us, grown up or not.

We don't hang on. That wouldn't be right.
They know we're here if they ever need us...
but I can't discuss that. Try to ignore it.
Thank goodness he's happy to keep it quiet.

It's not a problem. His friend is welcome.
A nice lad, almost another son I suppose.
I couldn't take them tea in bed though.
(I always took him tea in bed...)

The only sign. I hope he didn't notice.

MARTIN HUMPHRIES

Brother Talk

for Carl, who told me the story

Slow, it began slow, with anger.
Anger comes not easily to us,
White, Middle-class, English
Who often feel sorry
but do nothing
Who often feel pity
but do nothing
Who often feel apart
but do nothing
And suffer some (though we're
awful good at pretending otherwise).
We've heard the stories
                              and sighed
We've seen the news
                              and sighed
We've watched the streets
                              and sighed
Shake our heads and move on —
Though each signal, look, gesture and death
Add up, slow but sure, they add up.
Then you — my trusted brother — telling me,
In front of her, telling me
how tight her cunt was
after all these years.
That broke my barricade:
My mouth opened and I heard myself say —
"Really? My arse and John's arse are wide open
after all these years of fucking each other,
and don't you think…" but I got no further for
He stood
She stood
Their two friends stood.
I, looking up, said:
"Though you are my brother, we are not kin,

54

though we share blood, we are not kin,
I do not have to share your mind, words or deeds".
Calmly I folded the napkin
Calmly stood
Calmly left the house.
I was shaking before I reached the bus stop.
I was crying before the bus arrived.

I was more myself than ever before.

The Sheer Mindless Brutality Of It

Family enter with ease
decide who gets what, those closest
rail at police for permission to enter,
when allowed are ignored, considered not there,
no part of his history.

This is our story echoing
through decades. Disregarded in death:
to us the telegram never comes, the deathbed
not ours to approach. We are made of no consequence,
returned to the shadows.

In death, as in life, we
cannot quietly slip across the river,
knowing family will reclaim, unless
we change it, gather strength, take action and
make known our wills.

JADE REIDY

Related To Silence 111

Alone
my pen rants to a blank page
rage at your actions
splattering in uneven lettering
along the lines filling space
emptying my head
of thoughts that turn
now to words you have not
yet read nor will for
you are already dead

You died Uncle mine
of a lung that shrivelled and hardened
had your heart shrunk too
I couldn't tell
it didn't show through
the skin that shoved
at my body in the bed
"He was a kind, loving man," they said
at your funeral I couldn't cry
for I thought it was me
who made you die
guilt rose in my throat
I choked on it smoked it
starved it to go away
for thirty years and now
the words splatter in uneven lettering
along the lines and
I reclaim what is mine
anger

CHRISTINA DUNHILL

Ring Of Kerry

This is the big one, ladies,
the battle of the bedclothes.
Look, in the right hand corner,
all our fathers weigh in their bulk,
draw up armchairs and bring
out the bibles. What's this?
Yours slips between us
and unzips his trousers as
mine walks away.

As soon as you ask me about
my father, I have nothing
inside at all, but this is
better than all that in my mouth.
'Don't put words in my mouth,'
you say. In your head are all
the words anyone ever wanted.
This is a homecoming.
We are so afraid.

Your pale eyes watch me quiet
like turf, smart as a parable.
Who will ever take care of us?
they ask. I, said the sparrow,
who am your lover and bold
as a schoolgirl. I know
the answers. I, said the fly,
with my little eye. I will
take care of you.

TRACEY CHANDLER

Rocking

That's my sister
You're beating.
That's my sister
Who's losing her baby
From take-nology.
That's my sister
You're burying
In an unmarked grave...

My sister sits
Overlocking in a firetrap.
My sister's blood
Stains the roots of a growing
A growing struggle.
That's my sister
Who is taking it
Pounding it on a rock.
My sister is crushing you
My sisters
Are taking deep breaths
To blow you away...

Ocean Blue

Come and dive into this blue blue
With me as it envelops body and
Winds around and between
Sneakin and snakin twistin
Round my secrets and depths come
Swirl and curl squirming wet in the
Sea of touch.

SENI SENEVIRATNE

March 8th - Belfast

The camera focuses
We stand
In the endless rain
With the endless graves
Under the endless gaze
Of British surveillance.

We focus on one
Grave adorned
With petalled remembrance
We focus on three
Lives lost
Now named in gold
Among the dead

We focus on one
Woman murdered
Two days, three years before
In a callous display
Of British justice
Dispensed through a gun
By a round of bullets

We lay a yellow wreath
On black marble
And remember Mairead
The camera focuses.

(Mairead Farrell was one of the 3 IRA volunteers murdered by SAS troops in Gibraltar on March 6th 1988)

MAYA CHOWDHRY

Desert Flowers

I was a girl
in a red sari
stained blood red
by your colonial past.

I was a girl
in purple flowers
adding colour to the dry dust
of the Rajistani desert.

I made a journey
where the blood
met the desert
and re-wrote my history.

DINYAR GODREJ

Everything is agreed upon, like some tragedy —
then the next morning in the same house,
everything must be agreed upon again.

He is now familiar as a bathrobe
doffed, as turning handfuls of bright metal,
I walk into regulated rain:

Where a knee's shine surprises me completely
as something I thought I'd forgotten.
I smile until I don't notice.

Things linger around me —
the breakfast table, newspapers,
four equidistant plants, sad cushions —

Until I walk from this possesive house
to stand out back and watch the sky, immense
for no particular reason, and also blue.

A Strange Music

A strange music as of birds roused from sleep
First heard when first I slipped into the night
Passing on a wave of intricate impulse only mine
That drove me past pavements lit, the virgin lights,
Into grounds where the hunt begins at love's doorstep
And a stranger's hands in the dark become a face
Defining what is known but never expressed, kept secret
As the moistness of grass, known but never expressed
As strange music of birds rising from the deep.

Golden

It's clear today we're figures of glass
in which a little amber liquid slides
perpetually.

On a day like this, sun-kissed,
water pours over rocks
always easy

an image pure as a calla lily
blown-up cool by coursing sap.
Fatal

this loving, lingering light,
thoughts without rubric,
still rotors.

A child, waking, yawns a wound.
It's surrounded, quickly, by glassy care —
pat

its blanket, lull its little ears.
Happy in our golden element, let nothing
tip us.

Emptied

After love, emptied, my lover settles
Around himself, eyes shut, a hand
On his chest. Were it not
For my fidgeting he'd sleep
Immediately. Even now
What thoughts does he lull himself
With, intolerant of the prickle
Of words, my ruffling touch?
And this from him who said,
Kiss me, kiss me, and swam
In my eyes. No matter, that
was the kernel, this the shell,
My lover is becoming man again.

TINA KENDALL

games

i do not care to toss heads you
win tails her answer no lie answer
do not care to kick boulders
that line my till now chosen route

turquoise pink creamy sun
rise greets your leaving all
day long feel you going then gone
i find myself sore and aching
from scarlet smile days easing me
to calm places where i want to reside

but cannot so i wonder
when does the eclipse end
sun shift from the moon
too many cogs in the moon
and how do the stars keep
dropping new colours i
get giddy at night spotting

them though my eyes do not own
the same greed the same trust
the same steadiness now

i know i must not look to you
for oil on troubled conscience
truth carves me up a crazy
ruthless dog i've loved turned
savage and then put down
then lie against smooth
floorboards mourning

i do not care to toss heads you
win tails her waiting to understand
exactly what i need feel want and getting
giddy watching starlight quiver

JOANNE WINNING

Pockets Full Of Stones
To Virginia Woolf

Your voice

Distills to one drop only

Spoken
Across the years of silence
which blind between us,
And the oceans of Time
Rolling inexorably in until
my eyes can see them only as
The Waves of Fate.

The animal scream of you,
Howling down the wires of our connection,
with pockets full of stones...
"I am a woman from whom the world was taken"

And yet,

In the night
Under a cautious moon,
I have plunged the Rodmell pond
Thrusting deep with woman's limbs
And finding your weighted body
Worked with crazy speed
To free you from the rocks,
Then
In the fierceness of the resurrection
Pushed us upwards, with a woman's strength
Until we burst into the air like lions
My arms around your weaker body
Water cascading back to itself from gulping forms

And then I have looked up and seen
The moon triumphant at last
To see your world returned.

JEANNIE BREHAUT

The Fire Outside

Night workers on bicycles fall from waterloo bridge
a trail of stars
she curves behind on her own time
the almost jobless waitress
Picks up her speed with no pedals over cardboard city
Leans down into the heart of it & sees a homeless man set on fire
   his house

She has a room she rents almost run out
holes in the soles of her only shoes
but a history of hope   everything will be all right
this week her luck is what she believes
when the fire engines glide near there is no siren
People burning the cardboard boxes they live in
not worth saving really
the spirit of the fire
is what the firemen are here to put out

Will the waitress see enough to write a poem
earn enough to buy new shoes
no way   in the end
the fire trucks won't put out the fire
police fill up all the holes
under cover of darkness
shake up & scatter the matchbox people
Five years is a long time to be anybody
begging & angry   she gets on her bike

The waitress understands the power of money
cycling home   her shoes   her bicycle
the brilliant flames a memory
If universal love came to her right now it would be money on
   the ground
tips people forgot to give her

the waitress is happy

PAUL BOAKYE

2000 Seasons

We are not a people of yesterday. Ask when first
a Brother's lips kissed a Brother's mouth.
We are not a people of the destroyer's world,
our roots return to Anoa.

There by the banks of the sacred Pra we met.
Before Ghana became just a distant memory.
Before the desert became desert. In that fabulous
Black time when poets among us still sang songs
of praise to the spirit of Brotherhood holding
our people together.

Under the shade of a young Nim tree we slept,
while the prophet Densua pictured a time:
The destroyers would come, nail our soil to
humiliation, and hurl Our Way into defeat and
obscurity.

Where in dream or awake I think of you. In
days two thousand seasons past, our feet roamed
freely through golden Ghana soil, our hearts
flew up high with birds on a Ghana breeze.
You loved me then.

Of my tortured enslavement from **THE WAY**, you
must of heard the stories told. I bear some
scars but time has changed me none. I love you
now as then. Will we meet and love again?

Or is our love forever tainted by the historic
chain of events since then? I have never lost
hope completely. Don't you despair. This young
black man still in search of his African Prince.

ELIZABETH CAROLA

"Milk Anyone"

The topic of tonight's discussion is Battered Lesbians.
The lightings's sort of harsh, you note.
You think to make the tea.

"We need to acknowledge the importance of the issue"
— milk anyone?
"Not to be afraid to make the links"
— and sugar?
"We need an analysis. A committee. A public forum. A refuge…"
— I know you like yours strong, so here

When her arm flung across you in sleep
an almost itinerant tenderness
was the tie that bound you thinly to the world

When her eyes went coal and you waited for it
sudden 'that's it bitch you've had it now' unknowlable
shocking you only   into stronger resolve
to anticipate   be more prepared   **to get it right next time**

When violent misery was the air you breathed,
seemed to settle the whole estate in a fine, steely dust
and you lent over the balcony quiet moments,
knowing it was the same in all the flats, women
putting up   shutting up   dodging blows   screaming back
but imagining a place   one flat maybe
where tendernesss was the way

You held this flat in your mind like a prayer.
And at night, half asleep, when you moved together
and her body relented   let you back in
you 'knew' you could make it   the one

The women are talking Battered Lesbians.
having nothing to say, you serve out more tea
drink yours   three sugars   slow.

SUSAN HAYES

Tribe

We are lost,
a tribe of orphans to the last
Lost.
We horde together
bind together
bind and bond and fuck together,
seeking the power
to kill the father.
The power over us.

We are lost,
a tribe of addicts to the last
Lost.
We horde together
drink together
drink and drug and fuck each other
to find some power,
drown the father.
His power over us.

We are the primal horde
the hunting herd,
but the father isn't here.

We stoke the fire
consume desire
feed the liar in us.
We come together
kill each other
kill ourselves.
The father isn't here.

ASPEN

When you wanted
to love me
you gave me
a chestnut
but now
i can't find it
anywhere.

Bitter and Twisted

bitter?
yes, i am bitter,
like acid, and
like poison fruit.
twisted?
yes, i am twisted,
like an old tree trunk
wracked and gnarled,
like old roots
twisting deep in the soil
i am here and i
will not be moved;
i am far too strong
and deadly.

EVE FEATHERSTONE

D.A.

I think I need adventure
Excitement, Danger.
Not that I don't have all that
Just walking home
But, in my spare time
When I'm not fighting patriarchy
I like to go Potholing
Climbing sheer cliffs
And riding my bike the wrong way
Round roundabouts.
Unfortunately they missed out
Caves and cliffs in our
Urban re-development plan
The roundabout is now
A gyratory system.
So I've taken up painting
Mmm, on hoardings, video shops
And porn emporiums.
My favourite spot
Combines my caving skills
With my new found
Artistic talents.
Thrucking under the double grill
Spray can in one hand
Bike light in the other
I spray Kill Men
Castration on Demand
Watch Out for the Scissors Chaps
All over the inside of the Gents toilet
Kilburn High Road.
I know it niffs a bit
But it makes me feel better.

('Thrucking' potholing term: *wriggling through a tiny space in the rock.)*

ALFRED CELESTINE

Inez Writes In Twilight

She flung my ring upon the floor,
Exchanging scorns, and went her way.
But I have tarried day by day
A cast-off lover by my own door.

John Crowe Ransom

April Year One

October: all day long
the tree outside my window
looks unwell, and leaves
a sickly yellow sail down
on strong currents of wind.

All day long the sun
whoops and dances in my room.
    The rain has stopped.
    I cannot bear her pain
    her soft adulteries of being.

    I draw on some thought
    at her altar: loneliness
    prays without caution,
    brings her to an intense pitch
    not at all matching my own.

    North east south and west
    her fixed stone of lust I keep
    all in alcohol
    and our secret is language
    and our downfall is in love.

All day long I suck
her fixed stone, and others see
the beauty of us;
others with nothing to say
put fingers into my mouth

put thoughts into her
and the beauty disappears
and the stone turns to dust:
    the tree outside my window
    looks unwell; leaves

    a sickly yellow
    sail down: all in alcohol
    the beauty of us
    and our secret is language
    and our downfall is in love.

April Year Two

She came looking back
at the edge of things she saw
    angels and demons
and if I laid hands on her
it was salt on bread   it was

looking back she came
on the verge of belief in things
    human and naked
and if I laid hands on her
it was salt on tongue   it was

unmaintained as days
when sin had its light sponsored
    when she ate my heart
and if I laid hands on her
it was not in love   it was

my choice and her loss
when my own inner being
    spun out of control
she did not pause to listen
but came looking back   it was

in my heart a thorn

and if I laid hands on her
    at least let me say
in a terrible happiness
I wish her the courage

April Year Three

In a hollow   words
between us were stolen goods
    when it is not rain
    it is wind   when it is not
    door   it is a pane of glass

when it is not light
it is moon   when it is not
I am receiving
stolen goods   it is I am
not the best word   but taken

April Year Four

We followed the guide
going early to the place
for a change of scene:
    — *Take the winding down of love*
    and it can become once more.

In her solitudes
the past will never be past;
in secret places
lives will cross one another:
    — *Take the winding down of love…*

I walk in full light
able to call on reasons
her heart eyes hands know.
I ask for her forgiveness
    — *and it can become once more.*

74

That is not to be
enters her every gesture.
Just as we cannot
close up the wounds the past makes,
we cannot keep on singing.

It does not matter
she knows nothing will happen.
Twice I tried to say
no one dies of spring fever,
and yet happiness was there

went without saying
"It was a mistake, Lucy…
it is a mistake."
The day slowly had filled up
and when evening returned

only one image
remained: a quiet woman stood
alone, patiently
on the platform, pulling
off an invisible ring.

CATHERINE BEGLEY

Close To Home

The only time
we have the guts
to walk down the road
hand in hand
in a busy street
Fingers enmeshed
to the bone white,
no space for breathing
or arm over shoulder
wrist encircling waist
is when we're drunk
and we don't care
any more
and in that moment
we live a thousand dreams
staggering and chatting
so it looks natural
to them
and i'm only carrying you
anyway, or you me
and we're two drunken idiots
pathetic, written off
until we turn the corner
watch and wait
careful, it's close to home.

BIOGRAPHICAL NOTES

VIV ACIOUS is a nail-biting existentialist. She cannot abide the capitalist-patriarchal-religious-sexist-racist-misogynist-homophobic attitudes that prevail in society.

ANONYMOUS is a 'female, gay, serving member of the armed services'.

STEVE ANTHONY Publication includes *The Gregory Anthology 1987-1990* (Hutchinson, 1990), *Take Any Train* (Oscars Press, 1990) and *The Crazy Jig* (Polygon, 1992).

ASPEN A member of Lesbianspirit writing group. Her poem 'Bitter and Twisted' has recently been published in *Disability Arts* magazine.

CATHERINE BEGLEY Born in the late '50s in a west of Ireland village. Is a teacher, aromatherapist and writer of poetry and short stories among other things.

MARIE BERCĚ lives in Manchester. Currently working on a futuristic novel. Thanks to Outlanders and Northern Dyke Writers for their continual support.

VICKY BLAKE studied at Oxford, qualified as a Solicitor. Now works in a warehouse packing books, 'dreaming that one day I will be packing my own. I dedicate my poems to my sisters Deborah and Letitia, whom I love more than words.'

ANNIE BLUE Born in Preston, Lancashire, and living in London. She is a full time writer and painter. Her poetry appears in *Whatever You Desire* (Oscars, 1990) and in a forthcoming anthology, *Wicked Verse* (Virgo).

PAUL BOAKYE has won the UK student playscript award with 'Jacob's ladder' and the BBC Radio Drama young playwrights' festival 'Hair'. '2000 Seasons' comes from his third play 'Boy with Beer'.

JEANNIE BREHAUT Born in Toronto, Canada 1968. She has appeared in *Delighting the Heart* (Women's Press, 1989), *Taking Reality by Surprise* (Women's Press, 1991), *More Serious Pleasure* (Sheba, 1990) and *Whatever You Desire* (Oscars Press, 1990).

ELIZABETH CAROLA Radical feminist, 33, ex-New Yorker. I teach creative writing and women's literature, edit, organise and try to sustain my old-fashioned belief in *sisterhood*. Published in *Christopher Street*, *From the Flames* and *Woman of Power*.

ALFRED CELESTINE Born in 1949, and grew up in California. Began writing at University. Has been published. Now resides in London.

TRACEY CHANDLER 'I love daughter Jessie, Mum Helen, Women Witchery, Rum, Raving, Growing, Grooving, Making love, Taking time, Oceans, Potions, Hackney, Harmony, Life, Love, I love Love.'

MAYA CHOWDHRY Her poetry is collected in *Putting In the Pickle Where the Jam Should Be*. And she has performed for Radio 5. Her play 'Monsoon' was on Radio 4 in 1991. She directed the Channel 4 documentary 'Running Gay'.

STEVE CRANFIELD Published in *Salt and Honey* (GMP, 1989). 'Probably the best gay poet under 40 now writing in Britain' (Pink Paper). Remains this side of 40 and urban.

PETER DANIELS Born in 1954, grew up in Birmingham. Has lived in London since 1982. Published work includes *Breakfast in Bed* (Oscars Press, 1987) and edited *Take Any Train* (Oscars Press, 1990).

ELEANOR DARE is working on a film script entitled 'Mansfield Park II' featuring dykes on motorbykes, masculine crazed Teddyboys and much damage to the upholstery.

MANDY DEE 'I was born spastic and was brought up as a disabled child. I'm now bedbound with Multiple Sclerosis. Began as an adult disabled from birth who also had progressive disease. Born white, working class, lesbian feminist, with anarchist tendencies. I have writing poetry and articles about disability since 1983.' Mandy died on 31st October 1983. Her poems are published courtesy of her literary executrix and friend, Caroline Halliday, and Caroline's daughter Kezia.

SARAH DELAWNEY 17, been writing poetry for some years, described as a deep, quirky, determined individual whose one objective is to get the most out of life, regardless of the prejudices. To clarify that – I don't give a damn!

CHRISTINA DUNHILL Published in *Rialto* and *Of Eros and Of Dust* (Oscars Press, 1992), *Stories in Wild Hearts* (Sheba) and *Sleeping Rough* (Lime Tree). Teaches creative writing.

EVE FEATHERSTONE When not doing vital resistance work in men's loos, she is sticking up the Law Courts and the Ideal Home Exhibition. She has been made redundant from H....y Council 4 or 5 time but still works there. She also has a remarkably tolerant teenage daughter.

JO FISK is a criminal defence lawyer.

MAGGIE FORD lives in Bakewell. A film/theatre director, actor and of course a hiking dyke.

BERTA FREISTADT is poet, story teller, teacher and now poetry co-editor. She only did it for her CV – but got to read hundreds of poems and met lots of women. If only all jobs were like that!

TIMOTHY GALLAGHER was born in London 1955. Works include 'Narcissus Goes A-Courting' and 'Just William' (Cicada Press). 'Barry Tells' is a section of his play, 'Minor Characters', first performed 1991.

RYAN GILBEY Studying at Kent University. He was the 1991 recipient of Kent University's T.S. Eliot Poetry Prize. He also writes extensive film criticism.

DINYAR GODREJ grew up in Indore, India. He has worked as a free-lance writer and teacher. A collection of his work has been published in *Twentysomething* (GMP, 1992).

BERNADETTE HALPIN lives and works in Hackney. She is founder of *Word Up* Women's Reading Cafe at Centerprise, writes comic stories and poems about breasts and heartbreak(s).

DEBBIE HAMBLEY Born 1972 in Yorkshire. Was Lesbian Rights Officer 1992-1992 at Manchester Poly. Now lives an isolated life out of choice. Her poems are dedicated to all her friends and to Caroline.

TESSA HANKINSON From Essex. Lives in Yorkshire. My poetry arose out of keeping a diary which turned into writing prose which somebody else labelled as poetry.

VALERIE HARWOOD loves to be with the sea, swim and watch the sun wave goodnight. I've been travelling since Jan '91 when I left Australia - and now I'm in London. I think I'll always be travelling somewhere.

SUSAN HAYES A playwright and actress. Her work includes 'Echo', published 1992 by Edwin Mellon; 'The Trial of Radclyffe Hall', runner up in the London Writing Competition 1991. She was born in Massachusetts and works at New Statesman and Society.

ROSIE HUDSON I am 31, live in South-East London with my cat, Mr Kit. Mr Kit does a spot of juggling and he's recently learnt to type. We both love the sea.

MARTIN HUMPHRIES is the poetry editor for the Gay Men's Press. His most recent book of poetry is *Salt and Honey* (GMP, 1989). He is a contributor to *Men and Feminism* (Routledge, 1992) and *The Achilles Heel Reader Part 2* (Routledge, 1992). Currently working with Steve Cranfield on a poetry anthology reflecting the realities of AIDS.

TINA KENDALL Even as a black kid growing up in a sleepy Yorkshire village, dealing in dialect, I used to get the biggest thrill from words. Books are a main delight; also cinema, children - movement into change for the better.

AT O'BRIEN Born in Yorkshire. His work is published in *Not Love lone* (GMP, 1985), *I'm Afraid This Time, Love, It's Positive* (Oscars Press, 989) and *Twentysomething* (GMP, 1992). He is the co-founder of The scars, a poetry forum for lesbian and gay writers.

RACEY PEISLEY A painter. My work is about fear, need and on a d day desire. This is a first attempt, and in many respects the first rait I have painted. Its publication promises to colour the rest of my

REIDY Born in 1962 in Aotearoa, raised with an itch to travel and She has written a novel, short stories and many poems. Is primarily mance poet.

EYNOLDS Born in Bristol 1965. Appeared in films 'Bailed of

Reading Gaol' and 'Flames of Passion'. Plays in band The Sun Tribe.

MICHAEL RUSSOFF A student at Goldsmiths College, London. He spends a great deal of time avoiding what little work they give him.

KRISH SADHANA I wrote my best poetry at eight years old, secretly by the light of an alo street lamp, late at night. Now I don't have to hide, poetry still feels mysterious and special but the orange street lights of nowadays just don't capture the moment.

HELEN SALKIN is always Jewish, occasionally English. Likes strong coffee, strong vodka and strong women. She dreams of a homeland and lives in Hackney. She wishes for Barbara Pym's equanimity.

JAN SELLERS works in adult education, gives poetry performances and teaches women's creative writing courses at Goldsmiths College and for the Workers Educational Association.

DAVID SEMPLE Born in Belfast in 1969, and has worked as a care assistant, teacher, actor and playwright. He now lives with his unspeakable Italian boyfriend.

SENI SENEVIRATNE Born in Yorkshire in 1951 to an English mother and Sri Lankan father. I live in Sheffield with my daughter. I love writing, performing my work, running workshops and singing.

LIANNE SNOW Graduate, gardener, dyke-who-writes, painter of The Goddess in a context of Lesbian experience. Born 1946, lives in Inner London.

NANCY WHITE is Scots by adoption and leads a life divided between lipstick and hiking boots.

JOANNE WINNING Virginia Woolf implored us to 'think back through our mothers' and to reclaim our history wherever we may find it. It was in this spirit that 'Pockets Full of Stones' was written.

GREGORY WOODS was born in Cairo in 1953. He teaches at Nottingham Polytechnic. Author of *Articulate Flesh: Male Homo-eroticism in Modern Poetry* (Yale University Press, 1987). His first collection of gay poems, *We Have The Melon* is published by Carcanet (1992).

PETER WYLES 28, lives in Hertfordshire. He returned to poetry Spring 1990, and came out shortly afterwards.